glitter books

ELVIS 2000

Jay Gould

ISBN 1-902588-02-9

Published by The Glitterbooks of London.

Copyright © Jay Gould 1999

All world rights reserved

ELVIS 2000

JAY GOULD

Author's Note:

This work was dictated to me by Elvis Aron Presley in the course of forty or more psychic visitations. As a renowned medium I have taken it on myself to translate the code through which Elvis communicated into my own expression of language. The code dictations are the exclusive property of the Church of Elvis, and will only be revealed after his return in August 2000.

—Jay Gould

CONTENTS

1. Prologue — 7
2. Hidden Recordings — 25
3. Life On Mars — 45
4. Angels On Earth — 53
5. New Recipes — 61
6. Jack The Ripper — 67
7. Extraterrestrials — 73
8. Church Of Elvis Presley — 81
9. Hitler's Post-Nazi UFO — 91
10. Illegitimate Children — 99
11. Atlantis And Catastrophe — 109
12. How I Died — 119
13. White House Secrets — 127
14. Crop Circles — 137
15. Jackie Kennedy — 147
16. My Secret Will — 151

I

Prologue

I was born at about four in the morning of January 8, 1935, a mere thirty-five minutes after the delivery of my stillborn twin, Jesse Garon Presley. On the day of my birth a bright blue star was seen shining over East Tupelo as a sign of my being the chosen one. Whenever a prophet is born, there is always a star attendant on his coming. If grief due to the death of my twin brother was to be my unconscious inheritance, then love was to prove my consoler. In my Mama I found the greatest love I have ever known, both in my time on Earth and in my new life in Heaven. Right from the start I was aware that like Jesus I had to die young in order to redeem mankind. And like Jesus I was born into a poor family. We lived in a two-room shotgun shack, and when I was two my father was sent away to prison for eight months in Parchman Farm. I would sit on the porch crying my eyes out, and then run to Mama for comfort. Gladys was everything to me. She kept me separate from the neighbourhood gang, and by way of comforting her for our poverty, I would say: 'Don't you worry none, Baby. When I grow up, I'm going to buy you a fine house and pay everything you owe at the grocery store and get two Cadillacs – one for you and

Daddy, and one for me.'

I knew already that I would provide for my family, and that the huge wealth I would come to acquire would be the symbol of my good fortune. I may have been brought up with holes in my shoes, but the road I was to travel was made of gold. I sang some with my folks in the Assembly of God church choir but it was a small church, so you couldn't sing too loud. I would trio with my mother and father as part of the same congregation. It was when I was singing that I felt right. I had this awareness that through my voice I had connected with my dream. I found a kind of peace in the music, and a sense of being whole within the space it provided. When I sang the world disappeared, and I was conscious of being in God's presence. I still sing each day with an increased perfection which will astound my followers when I return to Earth in the year 2000. I have prepared myself for the second coming, and will in a later chapter give you details of some of the new material I have recorded, and which will be released next year to coincide with my return. Gladys has heard all the new songs and I continue to grow in the light of her encouragement. Amen.

I want to comfort you all by saying that each person has a place on Earth. The humbleness of my origins in no way detracted from my mission. I knew right from the start what I had to do, and when at the age of ten I surprised Gladys by standing up and singing in front of an audience of several hundred at the Mississippi-Alabama Fair and Dairy Show at the Fairgrounds in the middle of downtown Tupelo, I was shining a light for individual destiny. I wasn't singing just for myself, but also to show folks that we must be courageous in affirming who we are. The spirit was with me when I sang that day. I was a shy, awkward kid in glasses, who you wouldn't have thought had the potential in him to be King. And soon after that I entered a talent show at the Fairgrounds, and with no accompaniment won a high place in this State talent contest. Vernon listened in on the contest on his delivery-truck radio.

After that triumph I got my first guitar, and learnt to pick out a sort of accompaniment to my voice. At first I played hillbilly music, but I knew where I was going in time. You can't jump time when you're in it. The ability to evaluate experience is always an afterthought. In death I've been able to reflect on the events of my life with extraordinary clarity. Everything I did led to my being the person who I am now; the messiah on the threshold of the second coming.

Most of you know the story of my meteoric rise to fame in Memphis, and of those early records I cut with Sam Phillips for the Sun label. Some folks put my success down to luck, others considered me to be talentless, while still others slandered my stage act by calling me a corrupt influence on youth. My dance was considered to be sexually depraved. But what none of my critics or audience knew was that I Elvis Aron Presley had anticipated every incident in my controversial career. Back then I couldn't have spoken of my angelic instructors without the risk of being taken for mad. I was visited by spiritual guardians and told everything in the way that I am now communicating to my fans through a chosen medium to warn them of some of the perils they will encounter as we approach the millennium. I am coming to lead my people at 4 PM, 6 August 2000, and it is my intention that they should all be there to proclaim the Church of Elvis Presley. I will bring peace with me, and also the music which I have recorded in recent years with my new pick-up group, the properly named Band of Angels.

Some of you have wondered why after my initial electrifying years of live performance in the mid to late 1950's, I chose to retreat from music, and as some have seen it dissipate my talents by accepting lucrative and in large part ridiculous parts in Hollywood movies. Critics view the progress of my career, after the messianic apogee I attained in the 1950's as one of slow and continuous decline. It is generally considered that the youth whose star had burnt as brightly as the one attendant on his birth had burnt himself out young, and persisted as a legend to his undying loyal fans.

    This accepted overview of my career needs some modification in the interests of truth. When Mama died in August 1958, I came back on leave from the army and visited her on the night before her death. She was the only living person aware of my messianic identity. We spoke for six hours that night, and Jesus was there with us in the hospital room. Gladys knew my life was to be a short one, and wanted me to spend much of it in contemplation of the mystery of which we were both a part. She instructed me to stop the work as soon as it was apparent to my following that I was the King. To overstate the fact would have been to undo the work. Gladys told me that it wasn't necessary to inspire people every day, and that I must guard the energies given to me as the chosen one. And so through the strategy of the blissfully unaware Colonel Parker it was decided that my image should cultivate mystique, and that this was best done by keeping me at a remove from audiences. I became a celluloid screen star, accessible to everyone but available to nobody.

In time I instructed my disciples at Graceland through bible readings, shared some of my mystic beliefs with them, and tried always to be an example of Christian living to my audience.

But often the destiny chosen for me seemed overwhelming. I took drugs because I couldn't cope with the dual life of being a rock star and a messiah. It was all right when Mama was alive. She would tell me that of course I would manage my responsibilities. She was a tough lady, who would give me a whipping for acting out of line, but like me she nurtured weaknesses. She drank because she feared losing me to the fans, and I took drugs because I couldn't contemplate life without her. I knew my work was also to be the cause of my death. And I wanted my death to be as painless as I could make it. Drugs were just one way of arriving at the inevitable. They were a sort of chemical crucifixion. If you are a leader or a role-model for youth as I was to the post-Jimmy Dean generation, then there isn't time to revise what you do. I had to act intuitively and take risks in order to liberate a generation oppressed by their fathers' war crimes. Of course I was ridiculed by the likes of Ed Sullivan and threatened with jail by local sheriffs for the explicit nature of my dance on stage, but I needed to make immediate impact in order to bring attention to my mission. I knew that what I was doing was epic. My producer Sam Phillips once told me in the studio that every track I cut for Sun had the proportions of filming 'Gone With The Wind'. I couldn't have done this alone. It was the holy spirit moving through me which allowed me to provide a new music to a youth culture.

The knowledge given to me in life, was however partial. In death, and by way of preparation for my second coming, I have through psychic communication with the renowned medium, Jay Gould, revealed some of the great mysteries which continue to occupy human consciousness.

I want to assure you that there is no death. When Gladys was dying, she said to me, 'Don't be afraid. Where I'm going is like stepping into the next room. You'll join your Mama later on.' I had arranged to have the pink Cadillac I had bought her parked within view of her hospital window, and as I looked out at it I was aware that 'Satnin' had no need of it now. I was broken inside, but I knew that she had spoken the truth. What Mama had told me shone like a column of light. I could feel its strength integrated into my spine. Of course the grief associated with her loss stayed with me for the rest of my life, but I knew that Mama had gone into the light and that I would be joining her there, almost as if we were going to share a hotel room together in paradise.

Prophets usually come out of nowhere. I was just another kid to the neighbours. A mummy's boy, who first found employment at M.B. Parker Machinists' Shop at thirty-three dollars a week. What I carried within me, although it came to be converted into money by others was an inestimable store of inner wealth. Contacts had begun coming to me when I was still at school. I would be sitting in the basement strumming along on my guitar and my dead brother Jesse would appear. I knew it was Jesse, because his name was written on the gold star placed on his forehead. He would come out of the wall and stand in front of me, even if there was a crowd of us in the room. At first I was frightened that the others would see him, but after a time it became clear that we shared a space on which others couldn't intrude. He would bring me bars of candy and place notes in my hand. I didn't have a clue as to the meaning of the numbers written on these scraps of paper, and then I worked out that they were references to pages in the bible. I would look them up, and little by little the pattern of my life started to fall into place. Jesse told me there was a whole system of contacts or spiritual hierarchies, and that I was to be put in touch with powerful guides. These were the figures I recognised as standing in the crowd at the time of my hound-dog performances, at the Opry and the Louisiana Hayride. Initially I had thought they were weirdos, and then as the shock wore off I recognised them as my own, for Jesse was standing amongst their group. I learnt from him that he had stepped back from life so that I could occupy all of my mother's attention. He had sacrificed his life so that I could go first.

Over the years I have grown to be the subject of worship. Scrawled across the Wall of Love at Graceland is an immense scripture written from the heart. You could call it the bible of the Church of Elvis Presley. The names on that wall endlessly erased to make space for new inscriptions are the names of those who will be gathered together on my return. The huge festival thrown in my honour, at which I will perform a new set of songs with the Band of Angels will also involve my healing the sick amongst my following. The concert will be followed by a meditational retreat in the Californian desert. My return will be accompanied by pronounced changes on the planet Mars, of the kind which I have communicated in greater detail under the heading signs. A major upheaval will occur in the overthrow of capitalist tyrants, and in the death of monetary systems. The King will personally redeem the poor and the suffering. The Earth is about to encounter the infiltration of Elvites. The latter are a species of aliens who work in my name. Elvites will grow conspicuous on Earth in the months preceding the second coming. They are recognizable by their gold eye pupils, and by their abilities to dematerialize on the spot.

As a child I would save up and walk miles to buy a burger, eat it and walk the three miles back home. I had to savour the memory of eating that burger in every step of the return journey, and continue to digest it like a snake for weeks afterwards. We were that poor. The Elvites have the declared aim of putting an end to poverty. As the new messiah, I shall like Jesus bring both peace and the sword. Begin preparing the way for me now by going out to the desert in groups and meditating with the mantra E. Be peaceful and light candles in my name.

As a sign of my coming Elvites will appear in Memphis, Las Vegas, and then in all the major capitals across the world, except London where the figure of the anti-

Christ rules in the person of Anthony Charles Lynton Blair. Look out for my gold Cadillac descending from the clouds over the Memphis Hills. I shall be accompanied by Gladys, my transfigured heavenly mother throughout the stages of my itinerary. In the words of the Eesha-upanishad, 'They have put a gold stopper in the neck of the bottle. Pull it, Lord. Let out reality. I am full of longing'.

I, Elvis Aron Presley am about to reveal myself as the messiah.

May peace and peace and peace be everywhere.

2

Hidden Recordings

There's a popular belief that I saw my style of music at first threatened and later superseded by the likes of the Beatles, the Rolling Stones, Jimi Hendrix and the whole psychedelic explosion which characterized late 1960's music. My flawless phrasing and sentimental ballad groove were viewed as unhip. Some critics said the King's golden voice sounded rusty.

The truth is I wasn't a reactionary to

psychedelic music. That I was raised in a gospel tradition and liked best of all to sit at the piano and sing numbers in praise of the Lord, didn't stop me experimenting in private. There are reel to reel tapes and studio acetates in existence of my experimental sessions which my management refused to release. The Colonel sat on anything which he thought would represent a departure from my image. I would fire guns off through the ceiling I'd get so frustrated, but I owed him my first break in the business.

But I was curious about how I could hold up against these new guys, and so I pitched in and had a go at doing psychedelia my way. I managed to get Jimi Hendrix and John Lennon in on the sessions, and Brian Jones of the Rolling Stones guested at the time of his visit to the Monterey Festival, where he introduced Hendrix; a young bass player called Elmore (Noddy) Flynn, who used to hang out at the Whisky A-Go-Go on the Sunset Strip and a drummer called Gene Aaronson. We were quite a unit, and to keep private about it all we would hire a small, no-questions-asked basement studio in Little Venice, and produce ourselves. We were there at Healter Skelter studios in March 1967, when I took a break from the shooting of 'Clambake', a film I loathed, and again in July and August 1967, and for a longer period in July 1968 when I managed to get a sustained break from the filming of MGM's 'Live A Little, Love A Little'. On that occasion we managed to get three nights in a row at Western Recorders, Hollywood, and two days at MGM studios in Culver

City, California. We had this lyric writer who was a friend of Brian Wilson's from the Beach Boys, and he'd write us any amount of songs. He'd give us his original notebooks, and they were crammed with poetry and stuff. He would write his work on the beach, and wanted nothing for it. I'm looking forward to reacquainting myself with this most generous of men, Larry Hayes.

Healter Skelter Studios, March 22/28, April 1/15 1967.

Sea Blue Vision
(Hayes/Hendrix – unfinished)

Diamonds In My Eyes
(Hayes)

Diamonds In My Eyes
(Deep Fry Version – Lennon on guitar)

Under Orange
(Hayes)

Red Confetti
(Hayes/Flynn)

Beach Party
(Hayes/Flynn)

Volcano Ash On A Windy Day
(Hayes/Hendrix)

Tear-Shaped Polka Dots
(Hayes)

Alice's First Trip

(Hayes)

Alice's Trippy Eyes
(Hayes/Hendrix)

Interstellar Nomad
(Hayes)

Dark Purple Shades
(Hayes/Flynn)

<u>Western Recorders, Hollywood, July 15/16, 18/23</u>

Sea Blue Vision
(Hayes/Hendrix – 1.38 version)

Love's Golden Temple
(Hayes – unfinished)

Black Pyramids
(Hayes/Flynn/Jones)

Valley Of Dolls
(Hayes/Jones)

Lunar Burger
(Hayes)

Lunar Burger
(Hayes: additional lyrics Presley)

Lunar Burger
(Hayes/Presley – Deep Fry Batter Stomp)

Over Under Round
(Hayes)

Stormy Blue Dream

(Hayes)

Martian Mountains
(Hayes/Lennon/Presley)

Blonde/Blond
(Hayes – written for Brian Jones)

Star Rain
(Hayes)

Surfing Leopards
(Hayes: additional lyrics Hendrix)

Surfing Leopards
(Hayes/Hendrix – Upside Down Version)

Drug Moving West
(Hayes – Instrumental Jam)

Drug Moving West
(Hayes – Vocal Version)

<u>MGM Studios, California, August 13/15, 22/27</u>

Rainy Ruin
(Hayes)

Auroral Rainbows
(Hayes)

But You Do (Baby)
(Hayes/Lennon)

Pink Sugar
(Hayes/Flynn)

Toxicology

(Hayes)

Toxicology
(Hayes – sung by Mary Ashley)

Deep Blue Dream
(Hayes)

Deep Blue Dream
(Hayes – Acid Attack Version)

Deep Blue Dream
(Hayes – Oneiric Vocal Version)

Emerald Falls
(Hayes)

Love To Love Your Love
(Hayes/Lennon)

Clouds Are White Elephants
(Hayes)

Death Boat
(Hayes/Flynn)

Pomegranates
(Hayes)

You Dream Me Up
(Hayes/Flynn/Hendrix – unfinished)

Blue Coffin
(Hayes)

Masters exist of all these songs, plus a number of home demos which I made at Larry Hayes' studio during the summer of 1968. I was bored with my routinal life of filming, and with cutting inferior songs for the soundtrack, and to save my sanity I kicked into what was for me unorthodox material. For a whole year I went freaky, but the Colonel was terrified that my excursion into psychedelia would kill off my loyal following. I played him 'Sea Blue Vision' and he threw a fit. He didn't mind me rocking with my guitar, but hearing my voice swathed in layers of mellotron, sitar, bells and synth was the end. He told me to get back on the screen, as it meant big bucks. He thought experimental music would be over in a year, and that we as a partnership shouldn't get involved. But I had the liberating thrill of laying the material down, and freeing myself from the celluloid routine which had been killing me for the better part of a decade. I was bingeing on burgers to compensate for my unhappiness. Being around Hendrix was a good experience. Jimi used to see visions of God in the Californian sky. He was completely psychic. He'd stop playing sometimes in the studio, and say Mary or Laura or Suzanne or whoever were making contact. He would go outside and listen in, for he knew the communication was important. He was the greatest virtuoso guitarist ever. And Lennon, when he wasn't tripping was good company, and could play anything by ear. He'd spend half the time on the telephone warring with Yoko Ono, and the rest concentrated into the music. We were all in trouble, and the work we did together was some sort of release from tensions, once it got under way.

Brian Jones was the oddest and weirdest of our studio drop-ins. The Colonel would have shot me if he had known I was working with such an effeminate being, and worse one who was a substances casualty. Brian would sit in and wait to be inspired. He might lie on his back on the studio floor and then get up and contribute some colouring to a song in just the right place. He liked adding sitar phrases to some of the more far out material like 'Surfing Leopard' and 'Drug Moving West'. He worked in little flourishes. You couldn't get him to play for too long. He knew what he had to do and he left it at that. He'd drift in and out of the studio in a dream, and you wouldn't even know he had gone. There wasn't the chance to get him to revise or add to what he had done.

The Brian who will return with me as part of the Band of Angels is a wonderfully transformed Brian. His spirit is pure gold like the colour of the hair for which he was famous. He shines on with renewed radiance. In Heaven Brian occupies a healer's role. His subtle energies are channelled into helping those with asthma, those who are depressed, and those who have problems with dependencies.

Jimi too has grown in benignity. His skills as a musician have increased during the years away, and he and John Bonham, two obvious rock'n'roll casualties, will feature prominently in my new musical line-up. And so too will John Lennon, whose flair as a songwriter continues unabated.

Our first concert will be played on a purpose-built stage in the Las Vegas desert. We will preview material we have been busy recording in anticipation of my millennial tour. Only I can return to Earth physically, but through me our heavenly music will descend from the spheres and be amplified through a gigantic speaker system aligned with Mars. So that you will have an idea of what to expect from the Band of Angels, I have decided to give you advance details of songs we have in the can.

Mars Is My Pillow
(Jones/Presley – recorded 6.12.98)

Psychic Graceland
(Hendrix/Presley – recorded 6.12.98)

UFO Overflight
(Lennon – recorded 7.12.98)

Purple Haze Revisited

(Hendrix – recorded 7.12.98)

Torch Song For Gladys
(Presley – recorded 8.12.98)
Crop Circle Tango
(Hendrix – recorded 10.12.98)

Bright Side Up
(Lennon – recorded 15.12.98)

Bright Side Down
(Presley – recorded 16.12.98)

See Planets Fall
(Jones – recorded 16.12.98)

Wall Of Love
(Presley – recorded 17.12.98)

Strawberry Fields Revisited
(Lennon – recorded 28.12.98)

Ecstatic Groove
(Hendrix – recorded 1.1.99)

Desert Blues
(Hendrix – recorded 1.1.99)

He Comes In Fifty Shades Of Gold
(Jones – recorded 2.1.99)

Rapturous
(Presley – recorded 2.2.99)

Moody Blue Revisited
(Presley – recorded 3.2.99)

Memphis Messiah

(Presley – recorded 4.2.99)

Church Of Elvis
(Hendrix – recorded 5.3.99)
Jesse's Star Song
(Presley/Lennon – recorded 6.4.99)

Graceland, Heavenly Mansion
(Presley – recorded 8.4.99)

These songs are studio perfected, and will be released as a double 'astral CD' in the autumn of 2000. They are without doubt my finest work to date, and extend the inventive skills of my musicians, Hendrix, Bonham, Lennon and Jones to their ultimate playing skills.

3

Life On Mars

During the course of my first Earth life fans speculated on the nature of the statue of me discovered on Mars. It was suggested that my Kingdom extended to the red planet, and that I was worshipped there by Martian civilization. Those closest to me and in particular Gladys were in on the secret of the Elvites, otherwise known to me as contacts.

Some of the Elvites were originally

inhabitants of Mars' two diminutive moons, Phobos and Deimos, and interplanetary travel took them to Mars. From the Elvites, and the King is talking technical here, I have learnt that the secret of life in the universe is buried in that area of the red planet known as the Coprates triangle. It's in an area southwest of the triangle in what is known as the Ophir Chasma that God has written his name on the face of a canyon. A transcription of this name was given to me my the Elvites, and was stolen from Graceland the morning after my death. It's a strange thought that someone is walking around in possession of God's name. This unsuspecting person is now a retired minder living in the Memphis suburbs.

It's been known for a long time that it's my face which is featured on the 'cliff' perched on the pedestal of a massive impact crater on Mars. If you study photographs of what appears as a humanoid face, with two eyes, symmetrical cheekbones, nose, mouth and chin, you'll find on close observation that the face is a representation of the King. This feature was the work of the Elvites. There's another reference to me on the 'DLM Pyramid', whose proportions do approximate to those of a human figure with outstretched arms.

Back in the 1960's when Larry Geller was teaching me mysticism at Graceland, the Elvites took my frozen sperm to Phobos. They assured me I would be the first father of an extraterrestrial child. By a process of artificial insemination the King has succeeded in seeding the galaxies. I have children on the Martian moons, and as the

Martians have the tendency to multiply by way of being interstellar nomads, so my genes will in time extend across the galaxy. Let it be known that the King who was born in Tupelo was destined to rule the stars.

Here again I'm talking scientific, but I want my followers to know that plans for the human exploration of Mars by way of a travel-light and live-off-the-land approach will be activated by 2010. You need to understand that unlike the dead world of the Moon, the Martian landscape features ancient canyons, dried river beds, the remains of frozen polar oceans, and enormous ice caps. I have visited the red planet, and I can assure you that fuel and oxygen can be produced on the planet's surface, and that an Earth species will one day terraform Mars and pave the way for sustainable life. I have walked across the excavation sites which are so prominent on the Cliff, and been transported up the access road which you will discover on photographs detailing the site. I have even gone so far as to promise that I will perform at the first out of doors festival to be staged there in 2015. Mars is only occupied for certain months of the year by its nomadic settlers. The part chosen for stop-offs is the Coprates triangle area, because it is near the equator and warm and sunny year-round. One of my interstellar children, a son called Gospel Elvis owns an underground mall there, the first big shopping centre to be established on Mars. Most of my CD reissues are available there as implant chips.

My return though will take place on Earth as it was my nurturing planet, and it remains of all stations in the galaxy the one singularly committed to the promotion of my music. My true family is made up of Earth people, and in death where we are offered the chance to reincarnate on any number of planets, I have chosen to keep my identity with Earth. It is there that I have laid the foundations of my fame, and it is on these that I shall build at the time of the second coming.

Still on the subject of Mars, my transport there was initially a gold-plated Martian rover, an unpressurized electric vehicle powered by lithium-iron batteries. In a very big way I'm longing to return to the ownership of a fleet of Cadillacs, the custom-built American limo being in my estimate the most exciting genre of cars in the universe. Gladys and I will undertake our

Earth reunion tour in a gold Cadillac laminated with a pearl sheen.

A long time ago when I was driving a truck in Memphis for Crown Electric, every time a big shiny car drove by it started me daydreaming. I always felt that someday, somehow, something would happen to change everything for me. I made the changes happen, and now I plan to do it for you. My followers will know in time the paradise to which I have been witness for two decades.

My extraterrestrial son, Gospel Elvis, will visit Earth to coincide with my journey to the East in early 2001, and will be the first Martian to announce a visible identity. Gospel will accompany me on my tour of Tibet, and later on my journey to India to meet Sai Baba, the world's divine healer.

The good news is that I will play concerts in China, Tibet and India, and that Gospel will bring a mastery to the lighting never before seen at a stadium concert. Look for UFOs circling the arena as I play. The Martians will set up a light display over the city in which I am performing, and this in turn will generate the immediate presence of crop circles everywhere.

4

Angels On Earth Identified

There's big conflict in millennial politics. Where I came from we worshipped the Lord with veneration. I gave back what I received. I tried to buy people the objects of their dreams: a car, a house, or some household thing. The Lord had been good to me, and I wanted to be that to all folks.

When I was a little boy, Gladys

would say to me, 'Elvis, you give to others son, and them angels will take care of you'. That was the voice of good speaking in a world which is so often full of bad.

Approaching the time of my return, the world is full of hypocritical leaders, men who are dominated by ego at the expense of spirit. Lawdy, give me individuality. I wore lilac ribbon shirts in Memphis at a time when this would have had you run in by the sheriff. Angels are those who stand outside convention and acknowledge truth. It's what makes Quentin Crisp an angel and Bill Clinton a cowardly asshole. Even Hell's Angels had more of a modicum of truth in them than corrupt leaders like Margaret Thatcher, Ronald Reagan, Tony Blair and Bill Clinton.

I've said, Mr. Gould, that angels are

those who pursue an individual identity. They redeem the world by keeping truth alive. In my case, I always knew that I would be recognized as a singer. It was that knowledge helped to get me through menial tasks like driving a truck, for the occupation had me temporarily out of character. I used to mow lawns to earn a little extra to help my folks, back in 1954.

The living relation between human beings and spiritual beings has diminished over the centuries to the extend that the bond of mutual development has grown severely impaired. I'm one of these who has come through for contact, and whose duty is to speak to the world before such a time as I return. In the heavenly worlds the likes of Emmanuel Swedenborg and William Blake were in their time on Earth in regular conversation with angels. Earth in its millennial year needs to re-open communication channels with the angelic worlds. I will make known the identity of a number of angels on Earth, some of whom will join the Elvites on the various stages of my reinstatement as King.

The humanitarian: Quentin Crisp
The singer: Scott Walker
The filmstar: Vanessa Paradis
The writer: John Michell
The spiritualist: Larry Geller
The couturier: John Galliano
The shaman: Terence McKenna
The archivist: Julian Cope
The explorer: Wade Davis
The artist: Joe Coleman

Angels as I have made clear are those who accomplish a task on Earth without straying from truth. In death they occupy what I would call a window in consciousness. It's how Mr. Gould you're perceiving me now, Sir. I'm a clear picture in your mind. You see me as a luminous impulse. As you will note the first experience of the angel is utter closeness. Once you are open to receiving the image, so it is as if ordinary consciousness were surrounded by another presence. If you allow the angel to stay, as you do Mr. Gould, then there's the sense of me letting you know constantly a sense of what you could be. Most folks have their mind-set turned off to the possibilities of angelic communication.

    I'm going to make it clear to my fans who are not into psychic experience how they can be open to contact with the King. It's as easy as operating a website.

Elvis Exercises

1. Sit in a quiet space, preferably your room, and close the curtains.

2. When you are relaxed, light a candle, and place it in front of a photograph of the King.

3. Close your eyes, and let your mind find a point of stillness, and prepare to meditate.

4. Now mentally type a code into your mind. The code you need to access me is 56565616. Repeat that number three times in

your head.

5.   After the third time the angelic image of Elvis Presley will appear surrounded by gold light.

6.   If you should have difficulty in receiving my image, then use the mantra EP as an additional aid to consciousness. You should repeat the sound on your breath as a form of vibration.

7.   Keep me near you for as long as you wish.

If you pursue this practice regularly, then you will be on the way to becoming one of my angels.

'May peace and peace and peace be everywhere.'

5

New Recipes

Nothing on Earth pleased me more than junk food. I succeeded in food-fadding on every harmful substance. Eating was my compulsion. Burgers, fatty meats, dairy products to excess, butter by the brick, anything bad for me and dripping in batter I consumed.

Immediately after I died I was an out of the body entity, and so didn't need to eat. But now that I'm back in a physical form awaiting re-entry to Earth, I've begun to experiment with recipes which I would like to recommend to my fans. When you've been dead for some time, and you're about to return to Earth you enter into a phase of what is called suprasensual delights.

<u>Red Ice Cream</u>

A specialty served in the shape of a sorbet pyramid and especially brought to me from Mars. Topped with cassis syrup, and made with redcurrants grown from terraform farming on Mars.

<u>Roast Peacock</u>

I recommend a peacock stuffed with truffles which have previously been stewed in a blend of finely-sliced bacon, herbs and goose-liver. When stuffed, the peacock is sewn up again and hung several days in a cool larder, until the whole bird has acquired the flavour of the truffles. Call it an Elvis roast.

Mojo Burger

A King-size burger in the shape of a piano with the lid open. The contents include melted bitter chocolate on mountain gorgonzola cheese. The marriage of chocolate with pungently seasoned cheese is one of my newest eating fads.

Symphony Burger

This one is a two-pounder burger packed

with a variety of meats such as chalons chickens, canards de Rouen, Southside mutton and Courland reindeer. A cosmopolitan delicacy. For the real Elvis touch, add a tier of melted butter.

Ice Cream Favourites

Blueberry cheesecake, soursop, cloudberry, pistachio Kulfi, crema catalana, and hokey-pokey, a luscious, rich ice cream studded with broken-up honeycomb or puff-candy. Also of interest are honey-chickpea and strawberry and elderflower granita.

Quintuple Goat's Cheese Omelette

This omelette is a new favourite of mine. Use 8 large free-range eggs, and a stinky cheese called Croltin de Chavignol. You'll note that I've developed a liking for mature cheeses. We never got those in Memphis in my lifetime.

Butt Boat

This is an irreverent dish for those of you who like ass. You make a mould of your girlfriend's bottom, and bake a rich chocolate cake according to shape. Decorate it with glazed violets or pistachios, and dress the cake in a pair of her panties. I ain't Mr. Gould, lost my sense of humour, Sir.

Blue Sausage

This is a chopped pork sausage, spiced with cinnamon, cloves, ginger and nutmeg, only it has been dipped into blue curacao. Suitable for the more decadent-minded of my fans.

My eating habits have changed from Graceland cooking to a more refined and selective menu. But I'm still looking forward to a good fry-up in Gladys' traditional style, when we revisit Graceland. I'll go for my six burger intake, and my favourite drink of all time, Pepsi Cola.

6

Jack The Ripper Revealed

I have met Jack the Ripper, and he has still not been reincarnated. The self-evaluation necessary to his soul will go on for a long time. He is in Hell.

    Everybody knows about the maniacal Whitechapel murders which occurred in London, England between September and November, 1888. The list of suspects has ranged from Prince Eddy, Jim Stephen, Montague John Druitt, through to theories of the murderer being a Jewish slaughterman, a Polish hairdresser, a Russian doctor, a Royal physician, and a woman called Jill the Ripper. At Graceland I would discuss the subject with the boys. We'd have late night talks on the Ripper, fired off I suppose by the Manson murders. Though Sinatra and Tom Jones had their names on Manson's death-list, even he revered the King.

Now evil is contained in the spiritual mysteries, and is a part of Karma. The Tibetan Book Of The Dead, one of my bedside books at Graceland speaks of the reincarnation of celestial or infernal beings. I'm once again talking scientific, but the birth-consciousness of a new celestial or infernal being makes for itself and by itself, out of unorganized matter, the body it is to inhabit.

The Ripper's crimes have imprinted themselves on collective consciousness. Some atrocities never get wiped from time, and of all serial killers over the past century, Jack has left the most indelible mark. And I suppose this has something to do with the mystery which continues to surround his identity.

Jack the Ripper was for many years a guardsman stationed at Aldershot. On dismissal from the army for reasons of sexual misconduct, he went to live in London, and took a flat at No 34 Percy Street W1. Largely unemployed, and living from criminal activities, it was his daytime itineraries around the city which provided him with a firsthand knowledge of the East

End, and in particular the Whitechapel alleys. His name was David Stanley. Apparently once hurrying away from the scene of the crime he bumped directly into a policeman, who unaware of the murder, simply wished him Goodnight.

David Stanley lived as a fugitive for 30 years after the last of his murders, and was never questioned or called into account. He was neither mad nor psychopathic. He married in 1904, but his wife left him in 1906. He died of meningitis in 1927.

The Tibetan Book of the Dead teaches, 'if men who have been warned by heavenly messengers have been indifferent as regards religion they suffer long, being born in a low condition'.

For many years Jack the Ripper's identity was known to the artist Walter

Sickert. In fact he scribbled down the name David Stanley as the murderer in a book he subsequently gave to a friend. The book was destroyed when the house was bombed in 1941, although the police certainly knew of the book's existence during Stanley's lifetime.

David Stanley, Mr. Gould, is still undergoing judgement for his crimes. Hell is in the dark, not the light. All of those who die – and I too underwent the ceremony – address the heart and say, 'Raise not thyself in evidence against me. Be not mine adversary before the Divine Circle; let there be no fall of the scale against me in the presence of the great god, Lord of Amenta'.

Gladys taught me to keep my heart pure. Be in the light is my message to you, or death will prove hard. I have made known

David Stanley's name as part of the process of divine revelation.

    'May peace and peace and peace be everywhere.'

7

Extraterrestrials

As I wait to reincarnate into human form, I can only describe myself as an extra-terrestrial. I always took it for granted that there are people from other worlds up there. I had close-encounter experiences from such a young age that it seemed perfectly natural to me to speak of E.T.s and greys to my circle as though they were an extension of family.

For those of you who doubt, and I

don't want to scare you, let me tell you that the universe supports innumerable life-systems, and none more so than aliens. Man has made the error of going looking for extraterrestrials with technology. The madness of expecting an isolated ship to encounter extraterrestrial life in the galaxy is something I will make clear on my return to Earth. This crude method which totally denies the subtle energies needed to make contact with aliens is as limiting as expecting a man and a horse to hold intelligent conversation. The two will never meet in terms of meaningful discourse.

Intersection with aliens occurs only through the union of sympathetic energies. It's a process which depends on psychic bonding. Contact occurs only if you are receptive to a particular energy field. What aliens need is spiritual and not technological rapport. Earth can send billions of ships into the galaxy and they will return with nothing but samples and deposits. Astrophysicists wrongly conceive of aliens as three-dimensional bodies prone to drop in on a two-dimensional world.

I'm not saying that all aliens are benign. Bad energy attracts bad energy. Abductees who claim to have undergone sexual trauma or gynaecological indignities as a result of alien contact are those who have attracted negative influences to themselves. Good contact implies attracting good energies. I've been down myself on lots of visits, and folks have sighted me everywhere from supermarkets to launderettes to sitting in a car outside Graceland. I once hitched a ride in a truck outside Memphis, and for an hour or more was in conversation with the driver about the subject of Elvis Presley. For a time I grew genuinely nostalgic about the past, and so stayed over and dropped into a local club and gave a performance of two numbers, 'Blue Suede Shoes' and 'Heartbreak Hotel.' At the time it felt so good to be the King again, although taking the applause I was conscious that I had to avoid being touched by the crowd. I was Elvis doing Elvis as an extraterrestrial. Next time round, it will be the King restored to his full glory who will enthral the crowds with full two hour concerts.

There's not going to be anything like a war between worlds. If aliens wanted to put a virus into human neurology that would be simple enough, and if they should decide on such a policy then they would target political leaders. You've gotta understand, Mr. Gould, that aliens aren't creatures confined to living on planets remote from Earth. They're intruders who get at you from inside, just like you're open to receiving me now. You call our world virtual because once again you rely on limited computer resources to establish contact with psychic reality. To us, your technology is an imperfect tool, a crude instrument designed to put metal into the galaxy. Humanity's quest for its neighbours in the stars is an insult to alien intelligence.

To put it simply, Mr. Gould, the King can visit you but where are you gonna find the King? If an alien wants to download data from Washington or Whitehall, it's an easy task. We do it periodically. The equivalent of the C.I.A. in terms of investigative alien intelligence is Starbuster Nine. This group acts as a watchdog on Earth governments. They're also known as the Blueies. We take human life seriously because folks have such an extraordinary capacity for pleasure. Astral sex can be ecstatic, so too can astral appetite for food and astral everything. It's a different range of sensations. Aliens are those of us who can re-enter human consciousness. I'm in that state myself as I prefer to reincarnate. I've been back to Earth so often in recent times that I've been spotted all over the States. It's all a part of my reprogramming, my preparation for the second coming. I like to come down and look at good old Memphis again. Sometimes I show myself, so that people know I'm not dead, and at other times I remain invisible. I often check out the grounds and house at Graceland, and sit in the garden where I used to meditate. I can switch my visibility on and off like remote. If I want the appearance of body matter I turn the volume up, or lower it according to the situation. At a mall in Florida I was so visible that I caused a riot. It was kinda fun to de-realise as soon as I was pursued, and I wished I could have owned to this ability back in the old days when the crowd would have stripped me naked if they could have pulled me off the stage.

In all likelihood there'll be a lot more sightings of me as the year 1999 progresses, for I'll be refinding my Earth feet. I'll be looking around old haunts down South, reacquainting myself with Hollywood, and surprise, surprise, I'll be dropping in on

Tokyo, Peking, Prague, Sydney and Auckland. I'll be sniffing these territories out with a view to performing there with the sounds of the Band of Angels.

I'll be back in a big way. This is my message to my fans and to the devoted Church of Elvis Presley.

8

The Church Of Elvis Presley

Some of you may be unaware that the Church of Elvis Presley was formed within months of my death in 1977. The religion inherited from my parents is best described as Pentecostalism, a sect which thrived on the persuasion of dynamic leaders. It was great stuff. We used to go to these religious singings all the time. There were these singers, perfectly fine singers, but nobody responded to them. Then there were the preachers who cut up all over the place, jumping on the piano and moving every which way. I learned from these people how to mesmerise an audience. These were my spiritual roots, but they were limiting, and through my reading and instruction I was able to expand and move on. The Church which has grown up in my name is very different from the Assembly of God church that I attended as a child.

The Church of Elvis Presley was visited by me in the manner that Jesus returned to his disciples as evidence of his having continued to live after his death. The church was founded by Gloria and for reasons that apply to the almost masonic secrecy surrounding members, I will not reveal their true names. It was set up originally in a Bleeker Street loft, and the rituals included active prayer, meditation accompanied by my music, the lighting of twelve candles, the display of Elvis memorabilia, the drinking of my blood, and by way of conclusion the reading of passages from a private journal I kept over the years – the book I called 'Spiritual Reflection'.

I had originally intended that this journal should go to Larry Geller after my death, for old times sake, but I was too ill and preoccupied in my last weeks to make this sort of provision. Instead, like most of my private possessions it was spirited away and eventually found by Stacey in a New York street market. Nobody really knew what it was, and the initials EP inside the cover didn't register with the bookdealer. The naively handwritten journal was thrown into a bin of two dollar paperbacks and miraculously retrieved by Stacey.

In this book I had set out the formula for my intended funeral service, only I had written it in 1965, at a time when I had no intention of dying, and had forgotten all about it. Stacey was to use the rituals I had proposed as the foundation for the Church of Elvis Presley.

It began as a church with two devoted members, both of whom are now Masonic Elvites, and while I have wanted to keep it small over the years, it now has an exclusive membership of 500, all visited by me at some stage and carefully vetted by the two founder members. In addition the church has a website, but access to my followers will not generally be supplied until after my return in the year 2000.

For private communication, when a tincture of my blood is used, Gloria and Stacey either wear gold lamé jackets or jumpsuits modelled on my famous Las Vegas wardrobe. For the information, when tinctures of my actual blood are employed in the wine, the blood is genuine. Refrigerated quantities of my blood were smuggled out of Baptist Memorial Hospital in Memphis, the week I died, and were subsequently purchased by the Church of Elvis Presley, due to funds put their way by my psychic activities.

The service always commences after the assembled have listened to a record of me singing 'I saw you crying in the chapel'. The sacrament is of course distributed from a burger prepared according to true Graceland style. Only advanced initiates are permitted to receive communion, and after partaking of me they usually speak in prophetic voices, like my childhood Pentecostal congregation. They find themselves singing my old rock'n'roll numbers, before later on quietening down and adopting positions in which to meditate. The service always ends on a note of reflective quiet, and sometimes I will make myself present to individual members. No service is ever permitted to have more than twelve members present. By joining my church you become my disciple, and I always had twelve of those present at Graceland.

It's intended that the true Church of Elvis Presley will become global in the twenty-first century. It has been necessary to nurture its beginnings in a small, individual way and to concentrate on faith in members, rather than on widespread popularity. The inner work required by me in order to facilitate the second coming has been immense, and my energies have gone into this preparation.

Of myself, I once said to a Memphis reporter, something like this: 'I ain't no saint, but I've tried never to do anything that would hurt my family or offend God. I figure all any kid needs is hope and the feeling he or she belongs. If I could do or say anything that would give some kid that feeling, I would believe I had contributed something to the world.'

Well, Mr. Gould, these are the principles on which my church is founded.

The rituals are kept simple, and the declared aim is philanthropic. My intention is to have people feel they belong to a new Earth. Memphis will in time be rechristened Presley Land, and there my people will live without the fear of political tyrants taking away their dreams and aspirations. I will rise to claim the nation's children. Rock'n'roll came from my heart and it ran over into my arms, legs, and hips, and spirit has done likewise.

'Though I speak with the tongues of men and of angels, and have not charity, I am become as sounding brass or a tinkling cymbal.'

(I Corinthians 13:1)

Author's Note:
This was reputedly one of Elvis Presley's

favourite biblical quotes, so sources who were close to him have told me, and it's interesting to note that he signed off a number of sessions with me by repeating these lines from Corinthians. I am reminded that his two other favourite biblical quotes were:

'It's easier for a camel to pass through the eye of a needle, than for a rich man to enter into the Kingdom of God.'
(Matthew 19:24)

'I will sing of mercy and judgment: unto thee, O Lord will I sing.'
(Psalms 101:1)

9

Hitler's Post-Nazi UFO

In 1945, at a meeting at the temple-like assembly room of Point 103, an officer of the Waffen SS was to inform the assembly that Adolf Hitler and his close compatriots had left Earth in a Nazi-invented UFO in order to escape being captured and brought to trial.

For those of you who are

unacquainted with the facts, I can assure you of their truth. Hitler really did escape from the Earth in a UFO or high-tech saucer. The incinerated remains thought to be him and discovered in the bunker were simply those of a common soldier.

Let me disclose the nature of the bio-machine invented by Nazi technology. I can only describe it as a ship which regenerates itself every seven years, a process which allows Hitler to live in an indefinitely self-perpetuating cycle. For the sake of UFO buffs and world historians, I will get scientific and endeavour to describe the process.

The regenerated part of the UFO is expelled by the remaining mother-nucleus as a new energetic circle of light, corresponding to a birthing technique. This new cycle enters on the same seven developmental stages, while the expelling principle rolls itself into a ball, which then explodes. The metallic remains contain particles of copper. Eye witnesses describe the explosion as forming a display of bright gold luminescence, sometimes with traces of rose-coloured smoke which condenses into greyish-white trails. At night the disks radiate in glowing colours, showing long flames at the edges and fireballish streaks of red and gold. Most remarkable is their power of reaction against pursuers, like that of a rational creature, far exceeding any possible chase. This is how Adolf Hitler has evaded capture in the galaxies.

    I have informed you of this in minute detail, as it is important for the Earth to learn of Adolf Hitler's continuing powers of evil. His craft is numbered 666, the symbol corresponding to the Great Beast of apocalypse.

But what the Nazis left behind them on Earth, and which still remains an actual force is an esoteric world-centre or headquarters of the ethically positive forces. The place is accordingly the Ultima Thule, not just of the Aryan peoples, but of the whole world. This was knowledge to me back in Memphis. Only a few know of its location, but it is not far – in global terms – from the polar base of Point 103. There are groups in communication with it through telepathy. The ancient Egyptians knew it as the northern mountain, On; while the Tibetans continue to call it Ri-rap-hlumpo.

There continues to exist on Earth something known as the Black Order, a

North Canadian hideout of Nazi survivors. Watch out for these people, Mr. Gould, is Elvis' message. They are in the process of developing advanced technologies, especially aircraft and methods of meteorological control, that will soon give the Black Order global power. It has a worldwide network of bases from which it destabilizes Western nations through terrorism, and the encouragement of racism and minorities intolerance. But above all, it works with the right-wing governments of Central and South America towards the eventual federation of that continent under its rule. The neo-Nazi Black Order will rise in South America and conquer the West if I do not intervene. The Church of Elvis Presley is engaged in occult conflict with the Black Order. My presence on Earth will assure the defeat of hostile forces.

But my warning to folks on Earth is don't be complacent. Serious infiltration is in the process of happening right now, and the Black Order – who are responsible for the laboratory creation of amongst other illnesses AIDS – are preparing new killer viruses. My return to Earth is paramount in order to help dispel the pernicious forces of neo-Nazism. A lot of my energies will be employed in giving concerts and spreading the word in Central and South America. It's my intention that Gladys should be appointed Queen there, and take up residence in South America for a number of months each year. In that way we will cleanse the Americans of the forces of evil, and make it impossible for Adolf Hitler to return to Earth should he ever attempt to do so. Psychic intelligence still hasn't ruled out the possibility of Hitler making another bid for power on Earth. He was in telepathic contact with Margaret Thatcher during her British dictatorship, and was looking to find a way back in by appealing to a sympathetic leader. The two of them had plans for death camps in Britain, as part of Thatcher's intolerance of minorities.

One last word on this subject, Mr. Gould. What Hitler fought was an exoteric war, and what he fights now is an esoteric one. I apologize to my fans if some of these ideas aren't too easy to grasp, but the King assures you they are a reality. Let me remind you how it's written in Genesis that, 'the sons of God came in to the daughters of men, and they bore children to them'. This exchange of heavenly and earthly intercourse has continued to take place in a way no different to the one described in Genesis. Prophets are born like this. My birth was the result of a son of God visiting my mother. The child she bore succeeded in becoming the most legendary person of his generation. In the next chapter I will reveal the names of my illegitimate children, both from my time on Earth as Elvis Presley and from the years I have lived as a son of God.

10

Illegitimate Children

Original sin was always big with me. I was brought up by God-fearing parents, and the ache in my groin at an early age caused me feelings of guilt and consternation. I found myself highly-sexed, but afraid of the consequences. When I first began dating girls I would dry fuck them, that is leave my pants on and just go down on them without penetration.

But later on, Mr. Gould, I more than compensated for my teenage reservations. It was only my wife who made me feel guilt and self-consciousness about the sexual act. I got to fuck the pants off so many pretty girls that you wouldn't believe it. I mean they would queue up to have me, and the selection was endless. I related always to a certain dumb type, naive young things who lacked emotional development, looked like dolls, and lived in awe of my status as the King. I've learnt since that the type I chose corresponded to my own arrested development, but it was all harmless fun and provided good fucking.

And let me tell you all, that sexual pleasure is approved by Karma. We on the other side rate it as one of life's supremely legitimate pleasures. Nobody in my millennial Kingdom will be made to feel guilty about sexual desires. Most of my guys were anti-gay because of their upbringing, and while the majority of the sons of God are attracted to their opposites, there are many who are attracted to the same. May God's blessing be with everyone. The King will protect all his people.

In Earth terms Lisa Marie is recognized as my only legitimate offspring. But as this is a time for confession, I should make it clear that I have other children.

In 1965 an affair I had with Karen Rogers, who was employed as an extra in the filming of 'Frankie And Johnny' for United Artists, resulted in the birth in January 1966 of a son Aron Jesse William Presley, who from birth assumed the name

Rogers. My fling with Karen had only lasted two weeks, and anxious to avoid a scandal I made a settlement to Karen, and a realistic one, which enabled her to buy a small apartment in Palm Springs and to have a number of years free of employment to devote to bringing up our son. It was the best I could do at the time. Karen died five years ago from cervical cancer, but Aron is doing well as a thirty-four year old lawyer, who also by the way sings and plays guitar in his leisure hours. He won't ever be big in this way like his father, but there's something there that's a recognizable talent. Without knowing it, he actually comes on a bit like the King did in 1958. No smiles, an occasional sneer, and some raw energy.

In 1967 I produced a second son through Sarah Vale, a girl I met while recording at RCA's Nashville studios, one day in Fall when I'd gone in to cut a version of Jerry Reed's 'Guitar Man'. It was sex on sight. Sarah was a mini-skirted, frizzy-haired groupie working in Nashville, who hung on to every word I ever sang. We had backseat limo sex in between takes, and out of that came a second son called Jesus Aron Elvis. Again I made things good financially, and continued to send money to Sarah right up until the time of my death. Jesus grew up as a quiet, contemplative kid, with a love of music, and is now a classical pianist doing solo concerts at small venues. He has dropped the name Jesus, as he was unhappy with the associations it invited and is a real loner who I look forward to meeting up with on my return to Earth mission.

Now I spoke earlier about intercourse

between the sons of God and the daughters of men as it is described in Genesis. This relationship is known as astral sex. Both the spiritual visitor and their physical counterpart need to share good vibes for this union to take place. Astral sex is a form of ecstatic embrace, and angels have been doing it ever since creation. It's also what is depicted in medieval paintings as a form of revelation.

    I've conceived a further two children through astral sex. Both of them are being raised within the Church of Elvis Presley, and will grow up to live as my representatives on Earth. They will encounter a world devastated by disease issuing from Genetically Modified food, and will witness the apocalyptic warfare of the new century. By 2020 the planet will be shattered, but my church will live on secure amongst Earth's ruins. My two sons, Adam Elvis, and Elvis Adam Jnr. will be fearless leaders in the nuclear desert. Both were conceived through the psychic, Mary Rathbone, a girl I selected for reasons of her possessing a benign psychic aura. Astral sex is as subtle as playing a stringed instrument, and can induce hours of ecstatic trance in the recipient. My vibrations entered Mary through her ear, mind and body, and so our two sons were conceived. I came to her in vision and she received me with her whole person. I simply said to her, 'This is Elvis, Mary, and I want us to conceive a son. I'm still the King even though I'm what you would call dead. Be open to me, and all will be well.'

That's how it was done, Mr. Gould.

Neither Mary nor my two sons have ever met me, but I participate in their lives through spiritual communication. I know their sorrows and joys, and suffer with them. There are things which happen to them which I am powerless to alter as it is a part of their individual destinies to encounter elements of suffering. We can't have the good without the bad. I'm not a watchdog on their lives, but I try to guide them in little ways, and to visit them in their dreams. The two boys are eighteen and nineteen respectively, so are of age to join their spiritual father when he returns to Earth. There I will father more sons and daughters, so that the Elvis lineage will grow additionally secure. My Church which was born of the Church of Jesus Christ will provide a sanctuary for my fans in the years of trouble ahead, and my children will from the arms and legs of the new cross.

'May peace and peace and peace be everywhere.'

11

Atlantis And Catastrophe On Earth

I'm coming through urgently on this one, Mr. Gould. The forces of apocalyptic catastrophe are gathering in a momentum which threatens to destroy the Earth. It's not just your political maniacs, Blair, Clinton, Gadaffi, Milosevic etc, these men are passing facts in the manifestation of the anti-Christ, it's the prevailing spirit of reckless violence in the air which so threatens the planet. There will be vengeance on man even during the time when I am on Earth establishing the popularity of the Church of Elvis Presley.

Now, there have always been catastrophes on Earth. For instance, the catastrophe which brought about the sinking of Atlantis was caused by the capture of the planet Lucifer into the gravitational field of the Earth, making it the moon you see today. At the time the drastic tilt of the Earth's axis caused many lands to rise and some to sink. The poles appeared where the equator had been and lands which had been hot became cold and vice versa. People have forgotten in attempting to assess the exact position of

Atlantis that the continent lay in the southern zone of the Earth, as did the country now known as England, for such was the angle of the Earth's axis in those days.

To know when and how things happened, and will happen, you have to be acquainted with apocalyptic cosmology. Today, Britain's Prince Charles is one of the guardians of the secret tradition, and as such has the title Helio-Arcanophus, Guide and Founder of the Atlanteans. On the other hand in Britain resides the woman known as Hitler's Daughter, who goes under the name of the Iron Lady or Baroness Thatcher. I can tell the children of Albion that Hitler's Daughter has a secret nuclear dug-out in Westminster to which she and the current Prime Minister and other associates in evil intend to repair in the face of apocalypse.

Beware of Hitler's Daughter. If she could get her finger on the button to release the biggest bomb ever invented, she'd be right there, Mr. Gould. And during his premiership, Tony Blair will live to inherit the title, Hitler's Son. Clinton is known to us as Callous Cock.

Now the angels are nine-foot in stature, so you will recognize them when you discover them amongst you on Earth. When they cover Manhattan, Paris, Zurich, Vienna, London, Dublin, Mexico, Rome, Berlin, Copenhagen, Los Angeles, Boston and all the major capitals, they will say to members of my Church, 'Go in peace'. The false ones who simply wear Elvis badges to draw attention to themselves, will be found out.

You gotta look at history, Mr. Gould.

When you die you get instructions in cosmography. The real history of time is guarded by angelic custodians. History books are just designed to produce chronological sequences of lies to conform with political propaganda.

Earth people have been through the motions of apocalypse many times. One of the most violent changes occurred when the Selenites, an intelligent lunar race invaded Earth. As the moon's orbiting grew closer, the Earth suffered from tidal waves, volcanic eruptions, then a huge catastrophe caused by the swinging of the poles, which also had the result of increasing the velocity of gravitation and speeding up the forces of attraction. Continents were engulfed, others emerged from the oceans. The equator, which had formerly passed through Siberia, now became fixed beneath Asia. The invaders, who were giants and armed with atomic weapons, had no trouble in defeating Earthlings, and in being acclaimed gods. These stories are part of Earth's inheritance, and we are in the process of experiencing the reintroduction of angels on Earth.

Again I have to draw on what may seem to you to represent hermetic knowledge. All those years in bed at Graceland I put to good purpose, and read the mystic books. I never doubted the truth they revealed, and when I died I discovered the true system of things.

In the coming five years, and I'm thinking of a period extending to the year 2005, certain major cities will be destroyed by the following catastrophes.

Los Angeles: Earthquake and tidal wave (2001)
New York: Viral warfare (2003)
Delhi: Bombed (2001)
Detroit: Burnt by riots (2003)
Toronto: Tidal wave (2004)
Hamburg: Poisoned (2001)
Brussels: Bombed (2002)
Amsterdam: Plague (2002)
Berlin: Plague (2002)
Pakistan: Burnt (2003)
Rome: Plague (2002)
Tokyo: Earthquake (2004)
Sydney: Tidal wave (2003)
Marseilles: Burnt (2003)
Auckland: Tidal wave (2003)
Moscow: Starvation (2005)
London: Burnt (2004)

When these capitals disappear, the survivors will form nomadic hordes looting and burning as they take flight from disaster areas. Earth will be the target then for interplanetary invaders, and the world's axial tilt will again undergo a polar shift. All of this may sound negative, Mr. Gould, but my people will be safe, and the Elvites will live secure from nuclear catastrophe.

Man's negative energies have been accumulating over centuries, and now they'll start to roll. I would advise all potential Elvites if in doubt to head for the deserts. We'll find you there, and the wide open spaces will provide room for prayer and meditation. Don't be afraid if you have Elvis in your heart.

Visit Graceland when you can, and write your devotional message on the property's wall of love. Every signature written on that wall is known to me and is also written on my heart.

12

How I Died

Controversy has always raged over the circumstances surrounding my death. It has been variously put forward that I died of a heart attack brought on by obesity, or that I took an overdose due to my depressed state of mind at the time, or that I was murdered because of my attachment to the Federal Narcotics Bureau.

None of these explanations is directly true. Yes, I was overweight: eating had become a compulsive habit, and as it was part of my individual destiny to die young I committed myself to this pleasurable form of self-destruction. And yes, Mr. Gould, I was depressed at the time. My marriage to Priscilla had broken up, I had big financial worries, my health was bad, I was living in dread of the upcoming tour, as I was too exhausted to perform properly, and most things in my private and public worlds had collapsed. You could argue that I lacked a reason to live, but that would be to forget the faith I had in my mission as the chosen one.

It is true that I played a game of racquetball with Billy Smith and clowned around on the court, played a few songs at the piano including Willie Nelson's 'Blue Eyes Cryin In The Rain' and got into bed at

8 AM. Ginger Alden was already asleep and I got to reading a book about psychic energy and to flipping through a new book on the Turin Shroud, 'The Scientific Search For The Face Of Jesus'. There are facts, Mr. Gould, as well as the appalling fictions invented by Albert Goldman to explain away my last days as those of a pill-crazy slob.

I want to tell you the real story of how I died, so that it can be made known to my people before my return.

It was decreed always that I was never to suffer physical pain in the process of dying. When I went into the bathroom, taking with me the book on the Turin Shroud, I had the premonition that I was about to pass over. I wanted to die alone and in a private space, and the bathroom had always been the sanctuary in which I found the peace in which to read and think. I had gotten used to calling it my office.

I hope you're receiving me well. I felt a slight slacking in frequency, but from your signal I can see that I'm getting through.

Well, Mr. Gould, I went into the bathroom as soon as I realised that Ginger was asleep. I knew that my time had come, and I wasn't in the least afraid. I wasn't sure yet what was going to happen, but I felt in a state of perfect peace. I opened my book and started reading. I remember being conscious of my heartbeat slowing right down, and my mind being very clear like I had never known it before. It was then that Gladys appeared. She was surrounded by bright light, and looked like I had known her when I was a kid. She said to me, 'Elvis,

I've got to make this little prick in your skin and then you're coming with me. It's just great on the other side. All your troubles will disappear, and you'll be appointed as a messiah.'

At first I could hardly believe it. I thought I was seeing things.

Mama and I had a little talk. I asked her how she was doing, and she said everything was great, only she missed me, and was sorry to have put me through the grief I had suffered after her death. She told me she should have been more careful with herself, for my sake, but that now we would always be together again.

This was a happiness I had never expected. Mama told me that we would be back in the year 2000, only that we would have a new house together, as Graceland by then would have become a shrine. We talked some more, and Gladys showed me this tiny blue dart which she said she would have to put into my wrist. I remember her telling me that I wouldn't even feel it, and that immediately it was done I could follow her over to the other side.

I could hardly wait. Gladys said, 'Now just think of Jesus, and we'll be there, baby boy.' And it was as easy as she'd promised. Getting out of the body is so simple, and I want all my fans to remember that. I took a last glimpse at my body, which had rolled on to the floor in the posture which it was eventually found, and I remember wondering how I had been able to carry on living with all that weight, and all the stress which had been part of my life. One little jab, Mr. Gould, and I was free.

Please emphasise the word FREE.

Gladys was my guide through that psychics like yourself, call 'the tunnel experience'. We travelled through the dark into the light. I regretted nothing, only that my fans would grieve for me, and be denied my recording new material.

There are some things about the mystery of death which I'm not permitted to relate. It was however made clear to me by Jesus Christ's divinely appointed emissaries that I had to prepare for the second coming, and that I was to be the chosen one who would return to Earth in the year 2000. This lengthy period of what I can only call psychic learning has been absolutely necessary for my development. My first time round I was too raw, too inexperienced. I was called away early to be trained in mystic affairs. I know now that the time is right, and that in presenting myself as the new messiah I will be letting nobody down. And I haven't neglected the musical side of me either. My new repertoire will blow the fans away.

Before this session ends, Mr. Gould, I would like to express a sincere thanks to Larry Geller, my first spiritual instructor. May blessings be with him always, and on the Elvites who in reading the scriptures are also reading my heart.

13

White House Secrets

It's official that on December 21 1979, I had a meeting with President Richard Nixon at the White House. It's true that I invited myself, in that my proposals to meet the President were viewed with suspicion by Vice President Agnew. Yes, I wanted the Narcotics Bureau badge with which I came away, but I had other more secret aims in wishing to meet the President.

One of these was that the President and I had both been having an affair with a girl called Lucy Drew. What I'm telling you Mr. Gould has never been made known to anyone, and in the fifty million pieces of paper relating to Richard Nixon in the White House archives, you'll find only cryptic hints of what could have escalated into the sort of scandal which in recent times has crashed over Bill Clinton's head.

Let me explain. Lucy Drew was a fan of mine, and while she came from Washington, she would regularly make the pilgrimage to Graceland, and had on numerous occasions attended my concerts in Las Vegas. She would share my bed, whenever she came to the latter events. Lucy died in 1995 from hepatitis, but at the time she was a curvaceous blonde, and so attractive that men would lean out of their cars and drool. Lucy was a hot little number in the sheets.

Lucy was a friend of Bev's, an employee at the White House. It was at an informal drinks party to which the President had been invited, together with Bev, that Richard Nixon first encountered Lucy Drew. Here's this girl of 19, and the President's making eyes at her and coming on like he's still a youth, and Lucy was blown away. She left the party with the President, whose wife was in hospital at the time, and ended up getting desk-fucked in the Oval office.

Well as you can imagine the affair got very steamy. The President couldn't get enough. As Lucy had always confided in me, she broke the news to me one night that she was the President's bit of ass. That took some believing at first, but once I was assured of the truth of the matter I promised to go and meet Richard and explain that Lucy didn't feel it was right that she should continue with the affair. She was afraid of being whacked by the FBI.

I was of course ideally placed to meet up with the President. Lucy knew I would be successful in getting an audience. I risked doing it spontaneously, and the request was accepted. I took the President a commemorative World War II Colt 45 pistol in order to win his favours, and once we'd got over the business of my wishing to help America by providing the FBI with information on the use of illegal drugs, I was able to bring up the subject of Lucy Drew.

At first the President denied all

knowledge of such a person; but I soon got him to know that it would benefit both of us if he was willing to talk. I placed in his hands the pink chiffon panties he had given Lucy, and the game was up.

I pleaded her case. I reminded Dick of his position, and of the dangers of an affair with a teenager leaking out.

All this was additional leverage to my getting my badge, and the President bent over backwards to facilitate this privilege, over-ruling negative reports on me prepared by his advisers, including J Edgar Hoover.

But I had still another reason for wishing to visit the White House and that was to get the President's signature on my secret will. My affairs were so involved and so fraught with rivalry from insider factions all hoping to benefit from my early death, that I decided to ask the President for his support in endorsing a secret will, the contents of which I shall reveal in another session.

Again, Dick was only too willing to comply, and with the fire popping in the Oval office heath, we got down to talking confidential. He told me that the job was an easy ride, providing you didn't take it too seriously. Vietnam got on his nerves, but the rest of it was plain sailing. He got some photos of Lucy out of a locked drawer, and gave me the nod. They were compromising shots of Lucy in her underwear, and Lucy in various positions on the presidential sofa. Richard suggested that they were better disposed of by me, for if they were to fall into the wrong hands there would be this massive scandal. So I found myself obliging the President, and reassuring him that the photos would be returned to their rightful owner and destroyed.

There was more conversation as to how best I could run the Beatles in, as they were known to be using experimental drugs. The President disliked the new wave of British musicians who were over-running the United States, and particularly the Beatles and the Rolling Stones, almost as much as he was an enemy of West Coast hippie culture. It was agreed that my position allowed me access to the pop world, and that I was well placed to be an informer and agent. What the President wanted from me, Mr. Gould, was the following:

1. Work with White House staff.
2. Co-operate with and encourage the

creation of an hour-long Television Special in which I would narrate as stars such as myself sang popular songs and interpret them for parents, in order to show drug and other anti-establishment themes in rock music.

3. Encourage fellow artists to develop a new rock musical theme, 'Get High On Life.'

4. Record an album with the theme 'Get High On Life' at the federal narcotic rehabilitation and research facility at Lexington, Kentucky.

5. Be a consultant to the Advertising Council on how to communicate anti-drug messages to youth.

What I gave the President in return was six typed sheets of white paper on which I had set out the premises of my will. This will is to my knowledge still concealed in the Presidential archives, but I will make known in another session some of the more significant points drawn up in that document.

14

Crop Circles

Crop circles have been appearing in cereal fields as a mysterious phenomenon associated with extraterrestrials. Having told you about mysteries like Jack the Ripper's identity, the location of Atlantis, and Adolf Hitler's continuing life in the galaxy, I have taken it on myself Mr. Gould to give my people an explanation as to why these symbolic messages are occurring.

There have been attempts to explain

away the circles as the result of minor local whirlwinds. Governments always do a cover up job on what they cannot rationally explain. There have been other theories which support the idea that the cornfield circles are being created by a rotating ball of electrically charged air, something known as a plasma vortex. Other people have proposed the theory that this Earth vocabulary is being written by ball lightening.

From a spiritual overview, these are ingenious attempts to give a rational explanation to extraterrestrial activities. Crop circles are a form of sky writing. We have been attempting to alert Earth to its impending millennial catastrophe, and crop circles have been a form of direct communication. This is an important message. My people must travel to these circles and study their form. Once you know how to decode the circle, you're in on the name of God and you'll be aware that what they tell you is like an update of the Book of Revelation. Go into these circles and meditate on my name in the simple way that I have described in one of our earlier sessions. Then the decoding process will begin. The circles are electrically charged. You've gotta think of them as being like CDs, and in fact some of them were like test pressings for my newly recorded material. There was an early one near Bredon Hill in Wiltshire, England, which was packed with digital information. We used that one as a sort of acetate or CDR. In that sense you can also decode the circles as a blueprint for a new technology, for each is a template for an 'astral CD player', and when constructed from titanium and aligned with Mars, the actual apparatus becomes a receptor for the heaven-sent music of my Band of Angels.

Crop circles are created by extraterrestrials, but in this case they are the exclusive work of an order known as the Watchers on the Threshold, a group of spiritual messengers appointed to watch over the Earth at the time of the new millennium. Their method of work is so fast that a clockwise drawn circle can be written up in under twenty seconds. It happens so rapidly and to the accompaniment of a high-pitched humming sound that people attribute the circle to wind vortices. A localized movement of air is understandably present as an ionizing charge. It's sad for us that people are so uncomprehending. They see only the circle and not what it represents.

Crop circles are like the open pages of a book to those who can read.

Now I ask that my Church and following make a study of the text written within a newly created circle. To do this you need to sit in the circle with the Book of Revelation open beside you. Adopt a meditational position sitting cross-legged on the ground, so that you are securely earthed. Hold your hands out to assimilate the electric charge in the air. Now meditate on my image as the new messiah, and use my name Elvis as a mantra. After you have been repeating the mantra for ten or fifteen minutes, a white light should swim into the mind. Now say to yourself, 'The Watchers on the Threshold are my custodians. I ask of them spiritual protection and the gift of seeing. Let me no longer be blind. Let me open my eyes to revelation and read the holy scripture written in the circle. May I grow wise on the message and prepare myself to receive a new heaven on Earth. May the divine watchers and the Church of Elvis Presley bless me at this moment and always.'

It's important then to wait a full half hour in silence before attempting to read the circle. You will remember Mr. Gould, the reference in Revelation to there being silence in heaven for the space of half an hour. You must observe this reference to silence in anticipation of seeing. What you will discover is not blades of grass flattened by a spiral wind vortex, but the brilliant illumination of a text written by the angels or extraterrestrials. You will in effect, Mr. Gould, have the keys to the heavenly city.

Now Sir, this isn't quite as easy as I've made it appear, but if there is faith and serious intention in the individual, then revelation through the crop circles is at hand. The circles mostly appear at night, after a hot still day, simply because the crop is best receptive at such time. The watchers descend in a columnar UFO, which some observers have seen taking flight in a trail of orange and blue lights. The circle is cut by the ship, the spinning central column creating something like a plasma vortex in which rising and falling air currents occur inside an ordinary heat-produced whirlwind. The columnar UFO then connects back to a larger grey saucer-shaped ship, convex on the top and bottom and measuring some 25 feet across and 9 feet high. This particular ship is often sighted, and that Mr. Gould is because it operates as a threshold vehicle, and the watchers make frequent trips to Earth from their spiritual station. To some UFO buffs, it's rather like train spotting: the same UFOs show up and they get to identify and keep notes on them.

To encourage my people to study the text written inside crop circles, I'm going to relate a passage which belongs to the inner circle. You'll find this text written in all the circles.

'There are four angels who will be seen in the sky on 22 September 2000. Their light will be known to everyone. This time circles will appear in the parks of all major capitals, and by the light of the four angels man shall read his judgement. The judgement made on each city will be read out by believers, who will avert the catastrophe in store for man. Then the grey ships will be seen in the sky as the Watchers on the Threshold complete their work. Those of you who know my message must leave the city instantly and head for the countryside. When you find a quiet field, then go and sit down at its centre. A circle will appear around you and that will be your protection. You will be amongst the saved...'

These Mr. Gould, Sir, are the teachings of the Watchers on the Threshold. May they be known to those folk who are my loyal followers. Elvis will sit in a crop circle with you one day, and sing to you by the light of the harvest moon.

15

My Secret Affair With Jackie Kennedy

In 1962, Mr. Gould, and this will come as an explosive shock to the American nation, I had an affair with Jackie Kennedy.

Jackie was in part living out her grievances against her husband's infidelities, and most notably Sir, the President's affair with Marilyn Monroe.

I had begun work on the MGM film "It Happened At The World's Fair", and though the project was filmed primarily in Culver City, California, the monorail scenes were shot in Seattle, Washington. I was on location there at the end of August, 1962, and it proved easy for Jackie to visit me at my closely guarded hotel suite. And for all her manner of formal reserve and fashion sophisticat, she proved a hot number in the sheets. Here I was, Mr. Gould, laying the President's wife as though she was a groupie, her black glasses and silk panties littered across the bed. A lot of people had implied that it was probably as a consequence of her lack of interest in sex that President Kennedy had taken a whole string of glamorous mistresses, but in my experience her orgasmic potential was inexhaustible. I'd have plates of sandwiches for her and burgers for myself brought into the room at intervals when we would rest. Jackie was always careful to disguise herself, and on her visits to my hotel she would wear a long blonde wig, and a style of clothes not usually associated with her public image. She would dress Kitsch, in a leather mini-skirt and crochet top, and unzip my fly with her teeth. But she was a real lady, and would curl up on the counterpane after sex and delight in reading fashion tips from the glossies. She'd send out for a slew of twenty magazines and thumb through them for the pictures and gossip columns. Then after exhausting the English language editions she'd send out for the foreign ones.

Jackie was a complex woman. She

had reservations about my music, but when she heard me sing the slow ballads she was won over. She believed at first that it wouldn't be dignified for her to be seen to support pop culture, but she came with me to the studio to hear me cut "One Broken Heart For Sale" with the Mello Men singing vocal backups and was won over. Her husband's musical tastes were schmaltz, but I won Jackie over to listening to certain areas of gospel and pop.

There was one time after an afternoon's sex, when each of us adopted a disguise in order to go out shopping. Jackie was a serious shopaholic. I remember her buying 36 pairs of shoes and a car-load of inessentials. She'd want a skin product and would buy one manufactured by every major house, sometimes just for the packaging or the name. She bought that afternoon at least 20 pairs of sunglasses, a variety of perfumes and scarves, toothbrushes in loud primary colours: you name it Mr. Gould, and she had it.

It was hard getting into her head. She was a silent person, except when we were having sex. But it turned me on to think that the President's wife had the hots for me. She used to like to buy a variety of bikinis in Seattle, and model them for me in the hotel bedroom. It was her way of having me admire her looks. I was forbidden to touch during this little game and had to hold off until she was through with the modelling. I think she was a frustrated model. She used to say that she would like to have experienced the thrill of the catwalk, as it represented provocation without sex. Trying on bikinis or clothes was her way of showing me that she was really a classy woman who shouldn't have been messing with a truckdriver from Memphis. But then it was back to bed and me coating her nipples with ice cream.

Our affair really only lasted during August and September of that year. In September I had to make an appearance on film sets in and around the Seattle World Fair, and for both of us the affair was never serious.

I haven't been in touch with her on the other side, largely because she is studying different fields of psychic knowledge, and we don't really have a spiritual bond. The political repercussions would have been huge if our liaison had become public knowledge, but I suppose that was the thrill of it. Jackie prided herself on good taste and I was proud to be included in her repertoire of the good things in life. And there was a humour too, Mr. Gould. The woman could laugh, and with some of the sexual positions we tried it was necessary to have a sense of humour. I see it all as part of experience. I contacted her soon after President Kennedy was assassinated the following year, and we spoke briefly on the telephone, but any magic which had existed between us was long gone. Jackie sounded icy and marginally stand-offish, and I had no intention of pursuing things. I had just wanted to offer some sympathy to a woman in distress. I don't think Jackie ever loved anybody. It wasn't her way. We had fun and then dissolved the whole thing; but I thought it would be good for my fans to know that the King held consort with America's leading lady.

16

My Secret Will

My last years were a financial mess. In 1973 I had been coerced by management into selling a lifetime's annuity from my catalogue of over 100 chart songs, and the money raised from this after tax was negligible. Most of my income in the last four years of my life was derived from the sale of merchandise, and otherwise generated by live performance. For a man whose earnings had been estimated as in the region of 200 million dollars, I was broke. You could say, Mr. Gould, that death came as a timely intervention between me and liquidation.

Now, it's generally understood in the chaos of my affairs that I left three wills, and the will dated 3 March 1977 was the one declared true and valid by the probate judge, Joseph Evans, despite there being allegations about it being fake. The latter will entitled my daughter, Lisa Marie, as sole inheritor of my estate to receive the lion's share of all merchandising royalties. As you may have heard, Sir, investigations into collusion and fraud on the part of my manager and record company were pretty damning, and it was declared that Lisa Marie had been deprived of money due to the self-dealing of my manager and record company.

Probably unknown to all parties was the will I had deposited with President Nixon on December 21, 1970, and it's this will I acknowledge as the true one. I'm certain there was a copy of this document in the office at Graceland around the same time, but nobody seems to have turned it up. Either that, or it was destroyed.

Because the document represents a true intention on my part to honour all those who I loved, I wish to make its contents known to the world, and particularly at a time so close to my return. The contents of this will may come as a shock to my daughter and living friends. In the will dated 21 December, 1970, I made Larry Geller my principal heir, together with Lisa Marie, and they were to benefit on a fifty-fifty basis from all monies accruing to the estate in my name. My close friends Charlie Hodge, Lamar Fike and Billy Smith were all remembered by me with sums of $100,000 each, and Charlie Hodge was in addition to receive a 5% annual payment on the estate's merchandising income.

Anticipating that Graceland would become open to the public after my death, as a means of augmenting the estate's income, I had asked that all revenue from this purpose should be divided between Larry Geller, Lisa Marie, my father Vernon, and my illegitimate son, Aron Jesse William. I had made provision for my second illegitimate son, Jesus Aron Elvis, in the form of his receiving the proceeds of certain royalty rights from RCA independent of the sale of my annuities in 1973.

I had made my first will at the time

I was dating Linda Thompson, and naturally at this stage of my life she featured high amongst the beneficiaries. In this will my 12 Graceland disciples were all to benefit from the residue of my earnings, and my father was excluded from the role of executor. It was a petulant will superseded by a second one in which I excluded all those close to me, and left my entire estate to Larry Geller and Mitch Wainwright, a car salesman I had got to like in Memphis. But both of these wills were destroyed, as they no longer represented my true feelings. The more I thought about it in those long days in which I would lie in bed in Graceland, the more I realised that the will I had deposited with Richard Nixon in December 1970 was the expressions of my true and valid feelings. It was always my considered will.

So, Mr. Gould, I can reveal to you and the world that the will dated 3 March 1977 is a fake. It was drawn up independent of my wishes and most likely at the request of my father. It would be impossible now to reverse its effects, but it is a fraudulent document. This should have been obvious to the judiciary by reason of the number of people close to me who were excluded. I was never so devoted to my daughter as to name her my exclusive heir. I will make things good in the millennial year and reward all of those who were excluded by my counterfeit will.

As this is the last of the topics I want to make known to you, because it presses on my mind, I will end these sessions by sending my blessings to my fans all over the world. I will come back to you Mr. Gould for further psychic contact, as there are still elements of the spiritual mysteries I would like to make known to those on Earth.

Even though the knowledge was overwhelming I knew right from my first raw performances in Memphis that I was the chosen one, but the personal realisation of what this really meant was often slow in coming. There was big blackmail in my life, and some of my huge earnings got siphoned off in that way. That, Sir, is another story, and I may return to you at some stage and make clear the identity of my blackmailers. Let me again point to my White House visit as a possible explanation. I of course went there to ask the President for some sort of help on a serious level, apart from my desire to get a Federal Narcotics Bureau Badge. I was scared, Sir. All this money and I had nothing to show for it.

When I return I will ask the White House to make public the full contents of my meeting with President Richard Nixon, as well as publish the secret correspondence that he and I conducted for a number of years subsequent to my visit. On this side, I'm busy completing my spiritual instruction, and I'm preparing myself to take on the responsibilities of being a millennial leader. Elvis will look after you all, and in particular those who are pure in heart. You too, Mr. Gould, my patient and faithful transcriber through so many psychic sittings must get ready to embrace the millennial changes, good and bad. We're about to enter an epoch of the world's history which will bring with it unprecedented terror and good.

My following will be saved.

Love me tender, love me true.
'May peace and peace and peace be everywhere.'

These are the divine words of

Elvis Presley